December

K. C. KELLEY • BOB OSTROM

The Child's World

Published by The Child's World®
1980 Lookout Drive • Mankato, MN 56003-1705
800-599-READ • www.childsworld.com

Acknowledgments
The Child's World®: Mary Berendes, Publishing Director
The Design Lab: Design
Jody Jensen Shaffer: Editing and Fact-Checking

Photo credits
© Alexandr Mitiuc/Dreamstime.com: 6 (left); Catalin Petolea/
Shutterstock.com: 13 (top); Clayton H. Sharp [Public domain],
via Wikimedia Commons: 20 (bottom); Dgareri/Dreamstime.
com: 23 (bottom); Epitavi/iStock.com: 6 (middle); Featureflash/
Dreamstime.com: 23 (middle); Igorkali/Dreamstime.com: 6 (right);
Imagez/Dreamstime.com: 19 (top); Jabiru/Dreamstime.com: 12
(top); JoseGirarte/iStock.com: 11 (bottom); Joseph Karl Stieler/
Beethoven-Haus/ Wikimedia Commons: 23 (top); Julijah/iStock.
com: cover, 1, 5; Larisa Lofitskaya/Shutterstock.com: 10; Michelle
D. Milliman/Shutterstock.com: 12 (bottom); National Archives:
18, 19 (bottom); National Archives NASA: 20 (top); Sergiyn/
Dreamstime.com: 11 (top); Stocksnapper /Shutterstock.com: 22
(top); timnichols1956/iStock.com: 9; Tomori Timea/Shutterstock.
com: 13 (bottom); Wikimedia Commons: 22 (bottom)

ISBN 9781626873643
LCCN 2014930703

Printed in the United States of America
Mankato, MN
July, 2014
PA02214

ABOUT THE AUTHOR

K.C. Kelley has written dozens of books for young readers on everything from sports to nature to history. He was born in January, loves April because that's when baseball begins, and loves to take vacations in August!

ABOUT THE ILLUSTRATOR

Bob Ostrom has been illustrating books for twenty years. A graduate of the New England School of Art & Design at Suffolk University, Bob has worked for such companies as Disney, Nickelodeon, and Cartoon Network. He lives in North Carolina with his wife and three children.

Contents

WELCOME TO DECEMBER!

It's December—the end of the year! But before the year ends, there is a lot to celebrate. Winter starts in December. People enjoy Christmas, Hanukkah, Kwanzaa, and New Year's Eve this month. Kids, though, probably celebrate a long break from school!

December

FACT BOX

Order: Twelfth

Days: 31

HOW DID DECEMBER GET ITS NAME?

In the old Roman calendars, a year had 10 months. The tenth was named for the Latin word for ten—*decem*. When the calendar switched to 12 months, December kept its old name!

WINTER SOLSTICE

The shortest day of the whole year is in December. On the **Winter Solstice** (usually December 21 or 22), the northern part of the Earth is farthest away from the sun. That means it gets the fewest hours of daylight. From then until midsummer, the days will get longer and longer!

Birthstone

Each month has a stone linked to it. People who have birthdays in that month call it their birthstone. For December, there are three (from left to right): tanzanite, turquoise, and zircon.

DECEMBER AROUND THE WORLD

Here is the name of this month in other languages.

Chinese	Shí èr yuè
English	December
French	Décembre
German	der Dezember
Italian	Dicembre
Japanese	Juunigatsu
Spanish	Diciembre
Swahili	Desemba

COOL THINGS ABOUT DECEMBER

- December 21 is the longest day of the year in Australia. In December, it's summertime in Australia.
- From 1647–1660, Christmas was banned in England.
- An ancient folktale says that animals can talk on Christmas Eve. Ask your dog!

BIG DECEMBER HOLIDAYS

Christmas Day, December 25

For Christians, Christmas is the birthday of Jesus of Nazareth, whom they believe is the son of God. The holiday has become so big, however, that millions of non-Christians celebrate, too. Stores love the holiday, too, since gift-giving is a big part of it. Big sales are held in the weeks leading up to Christmas. For most families, Christmas is the biggest get-together of the year!

Kwanzaa, December 26

Kwanzaa was created in 1966 to honor African history and community. Today, African-Americans begin Kwanzaa on December 26. They focus on values such as responsibility, creativity, and faith. Red, black, and green candles symbolize those values during Kwanzaa.

HANUKKAH

Hanukkah is an eight-day festival that is most often celebrated in December, but sometimes it's celebrated in November. Jewish families remember a miracle during which a one-day supply of lamp oil lasted for eight days during a long-ago battle. During Hanukkah, children often get a new present on each of the eight nights!

FUN DECEMBER DAYS

You can celebrate December in more ways than just by licking candy canes! Here are some of the unusual holidays you can enjoy in December:

December 4

Wear Brown Shoes Day

December 7

Letter-Writing Day

December 12

National Poinsettia Day

December 13

Violin Day

December 17

National Maple Syrup Day

December 20

Go Caroling Day

December 21

National
Flashlight Day

December 27

National
Fruitcake Day

DECEMBER WEEKS AND MONTHS

Holidays don't just mean days…you can celebrate for a week, too! You can also have fun all month long. Find out more about these ways to enjoy December!

DECEMBER WEEKS

Computer Science Education Week: This week, try to find out something about how computers work. Ask your teacher to show you how to write some code. Even President Obama says that's a good idea!

Christmas Bird-Count Week: For bird-watchers, this is the biggest week of the year. "Birders" from around the country spread out and count. They list all the types of birds they see. The Audubon Society combines the list. They report all the birds that live in the U.S.

DECEMBER MONTHS

Fruitcake Month: Fruitcake is one of those foods that you love or you hate. It's been a holiday tradition for centuries. The ancient Romans even made fruitcake. It can be a bit sticky and sweet, but you never know until you try it!

World AIDS Month: The disease known as AIDS has affected millions of people over the past few decades. In December, events are held at hospitals and other sites. Some remember the victims. Other events educate people about new treatments. AIDS is slowly being beaten, but it will be a tough fight.

DECEMBER AROUND THE WORLD

Countries around the world celebrate in December. Find these countries on the map. Then read about how people there have fun in December!

December 26

Junkanoo, Bahamas
Long ago, this was the "day off" for slaves on this island. Today, it remains as a day-and-night long party, with parades, music, and dancing.

BOXING DAY

In Great Britain, the day after Christmas is Boxing Day. People give small presents—in boxes!—to people who help during the year. Postal workers, repair people, shopkeepers, and more enjoy this day. It's also celebrated in Australia and other countries. Some think the name came from Christmas "boxes" given to servants on this day.

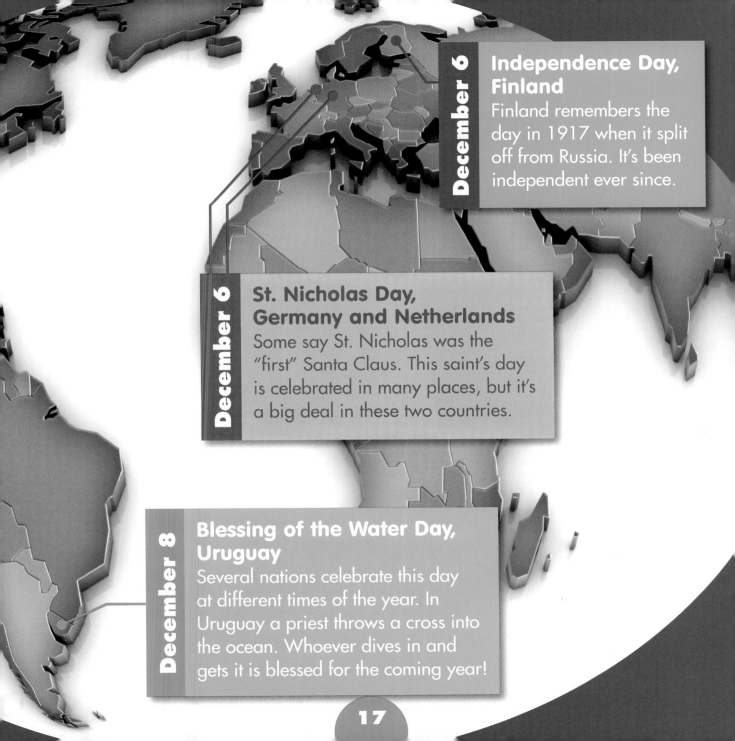

December 6

Independence Day, Finland

Finland remembers the day in 1917 when it split off from Russia. It's been independent ever since.

December 6

St. Nicholas Day, Germany and Netherlands

Some say St. Nicholas was the "first" Santa Claus. This saint's day is celebrated in many places, but it's a big deal in these two countries.

December 8

Blessing of the Water Day, Uruguay

Several nations celebrate this day at different times of the year. In Uruguay a priest throws a cross into the ocean. Whoever dives in and gets it is blessed for the coming year!

DECEMBER IN HISTORY

December 1, 1955

Rosa Parks was arrested in Montgomery, Alabama. She was told to give her seat on a bus because she was black. She refused. Her arrest helped spark the **Civil Rights Movement**.

PEARL HARBOR

Airplanes from the Japanese Navy attacked Pearl Harbor in Hawaii on December 7, 1941. The U.S. declared war on Japan after the attack. Germany and Italy declared war on the U.S. as well. By early 1942, World War II was raging in Europe, Africa, and Asia.

December 3, 1992

The first text message was sent. It read "Merry Christmas."

December 6, 1884

The Washington Monument was completed in Washington D.C.

December 14, 1911

Roald Amundsen of Sweden became the first person to reach the South Pole.

December 16, 1773

At the Boston Tea Party, **colonists** dumped British tea in Boston Harbor to protest a tax.

December 17, 1903

Wilbur and Orville Wright became the first people ever to fly an airplane. The first flight lasted only 12 seconds.

December 18, 1620

The *Mayflower*, a ship containing English Pilgrims, arrived in what would become Massachusetts.

December 23, 1986

The *Voyager* aircraft became the first to fly around the world without stopping or refueling.

December 31, 1879

Thomas Edison showed off his new electric light bulb in public for the first time.

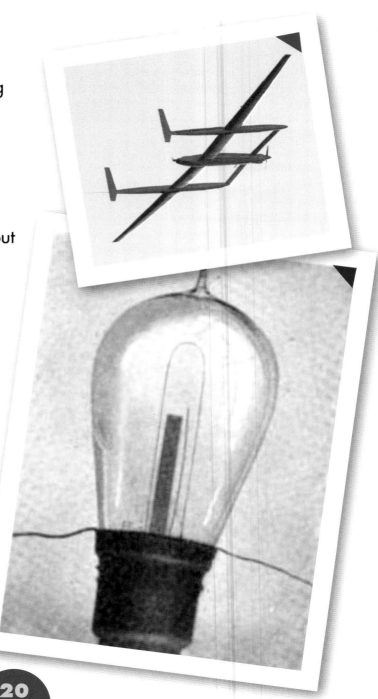

NEW STATES!

Nine states first joined the United States in December. Do you live in any of these? If you do, then make sure and say, "Happy Birthday!" to your state.

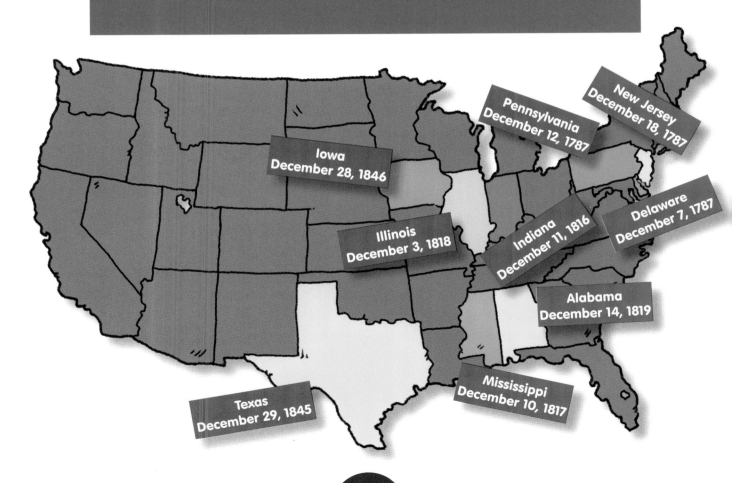

Iowa
December 28, 1846

Pennsylvania
December 12, 1787

New Jersey
December 18, 1787

Illinois
December 3, 1818

Indiana
December 11, 1816

Delaware
December 7, 1787

Alabama
December 14, 1819

Texas
December 29, 1845

Mississippi
December 10, 1817

FAMOUS DECEMBER BIRTHDAYS

December 5

Martin Van Buren
He was President of the United States from 1837–1841.

December 5

Walt Disney
A great storyteller and businessman, he helped create great movies and started Disneyland.

December 10

Emily Dickinson
Her beautiful poems remain among the most famous ever by an American.

December 16

Ludwig van Beethoven
This German wrote classical music and operas.

December 18

Steven Spielberg
This movie director created hits that include *E.T.*, *Indiana Jones*, and *Jaws*.

December 28

Stan Lee
He helped create Spider-Man, Fantastic Four, X-Men, and other comic-book heroes.

December 30

LeBron James
The four-time NBA MVP led the Miami Heat to two NBA championships.

GLOSSARY

Christians (KRISS-chunz) People who believe in the teachings of a man named Jesus of Nazareth.

Civil Rights Movement (SIV-ul RYTS MOVE-munt) The fight for all people to have equal treatment and freedom.

colonists (KOLL-uh-nists) People living in a newly settled area.

Winter Solstice (WIN-tur SOHL-stiss) A time when the Earth is farthest away from the sun. It is the shortest day of the year.

INDEX